THE KEY

*A Guide to Unlocking
Your Creative Power*

LACEY HAWK

Address all inquiries to the author:
ofinnerpeace@aol.com

Printed in the United States
ISBN: 978-1-68222-676-6

A special thank you to KasterTroy at Level 8 Studios for cover design, level8studios.com.
Interior Formatting by Penoaks Publishing, http://penoaks.com
Cover and interior images from Shutterstock

To my clients, friends, and family,
who have enriched my life in many ways.
And to the Power within us all.

TABLE OF CONTENTS

INTRODUCTION

A fter a near-death experience at the age of four I began to learn about energy. I could *feel* energy in a way I previously had not felt. I could look at someone and I just knew if they were kind or mean-spirited. I could tell if they were happy, sad, filled with anger, or ill. Of course, I had no idea at the time what energy actually was, only that I sensed things deeply. There was an inner knowing, and the premise of my perception was based on waves of energy; vibrational frequencies. Later in life I learned how to direct energy, and that is what I will be teaching in this book. Knowing how to channel your power and direct energy by focusing your thoughts is *the key* to effortlessly creating a heavenly life.

I have always found it an interesting term, *near-death experience* (NDE), when those that have the experience are, in fact, *dead*. Not near dead, but quite dead. So I prefer to refer to it as a *death experience* (DE), and for the sake of discussion only, as there truly is no death. Life is eternal, and death is simply a spiritual transition.

In 1961, after spending half an hour at the bottom of the ocean, and another half hour being transported to the nearest hospital, my tiny lifeless body was revived.

It was presumed that I had been dead well over an hour. I gather that this clinical death was not recorded in its entirety, being that its duration took place, in most part, outside of a medical facility.

Dannion Brinkley, whose first of three death experiences in 1975, caused by being struck by lightening, holds the record for being clinically dead for 28 minutes. Afterward, he had a very hard time recuperating mentally and physically. In his book *Saved By the Light* he shares, not only a lengthy, detailed description of his experience on the other side, but also the difficulties after returning, including learning to walk and feed himself again. But he also awakened to many gifts, and is well-respected for delivering inspirational and insightful messages all over the world.

My second DE occurred in my early thirties while in the hospital having an outpatient surgical procedure. I was having a benign tumor removed from my wrist, and it was expected to have been minor surgery. I was awake during the operation, and due to complications, the surgery ended up being much more involved. The tumor was deeper than anticipated, and the surgeon was going to have to cut into the bone.

An anesthesiologist was present, administering something to keep me relaxed. But when the surgeon proceeded and began cutting, I flatlined.

The anesthesiologist panicked, assuming he had given me too much anesthesia. However, I believe that I simply could not endure what was happening; the sounds, and the thought of someone digging around in my bone, so I exited, right out the top of my head.

When I returned to my body, the anesthesiologist was actually crying. He thought he had killed me. Poor guy. I felt so bad for him, that instead of paying attention to my own well-being, I attempted to console him.

I was gone for only a minute or two, but it seemed to affect me more than the first DE, both physically and emotionally.

The first time, oddly, I had no physical issues or discomfort after returning. I should have suffered extreme brain damage. The second left me feeling very out of sorts. I was nauseous and drained, and I had a difficult time recovering initially. And worst of all, I was not happy to have returned. This left me feeling guilty because I had a child that I loved more than anything in the world. But the feeling that overtook my out-of-body senses was something verbally indescribable, and I wanted more of it.

Dannion felt similarly. In his book he describes the euphoric feeling, and his anger at not being allowed to remain in the afterlife.

I once hosted a radio show that centered on spiritual subjects, and my first guest was Dr. Raymond Moody, leading authority of DE's, and best-selling author of twelve books including *Life After Life*.

I was a bit green, being it was my first experience hosting a radio show, and my first interview. I was a little nervous initially, but Dr. Moody made it easy for me. He was genuinely warm-hearted, and a fantastic communicator, which made my job, not only easy, but thoroughly enjoyable. He is someone I would have loved to have gotten to know personally; a very down-to-earth guy.

About halfway through the interview I shared with Dr. Moody that I had died twice. His response, which was not what I expected, was a jovial, "Good for you!"

I laughed heartily, but he was totally serious as he asked, "You don't fear death, do you?" My answer was a firm, "No. I do not."

Dr. Moody actually had assisted a confused Dannion with his knowledge after his first DE, and the two lectured together extensively on the subject at that time.

The year following my first DE I had my first of many encounters with Jesus. A couple of years after the second death experience I was visited by a host of benevolent beings that encouraged me to begin my true work. They were referring to my ability to heal.

I did as I was urged to do only a few days later, healing a woman of lymphoma, and have been laying hands on people ever since, worldwide, for over twenty years, curing everything from the flu to terminal cancer.

I believe it was after the first DE that the healing power was awakened. And I became aware that I possessed many gifts. I could see spirits, I could hear voices, and I could not only feel energy, I could also see energy. For me, everything is moving all the time. Even the walls have movement. There are colors and patterns visible in everything. I have often thought it funny that people who drop acid do so in order to have the kind of psychedelic trip I am always on.

The interesting thing is that it has never seemed abnormal. It has always felt right. As a child, and throughout my life, I never once questioned my abilities. I also never shared my unusual reality with anyone until after I began to utilize my healing power, mostly because I was afraid of being judged. People get locked up for hearing voices. It has only been in recent years that there is more awareness and openness to subjects of a spiritual nature.

Without going in to a great deal of detail, my first DE was due to drowning in the ocean in Miami at the age of four. I had been taken on a blow-up raft by my uncle quite a distance away from shore. The water was a beautiful shade of blue that day, and it looked like there were tiny diamonds twinkling on the surface.

My uncle was a prankster, and his intention was to scare me by slipping off of the raft, hiding underneath, and tipping it over. But when he did tip it over, instead of falling off close to the raft, I shot away from it, farther than anticipated, and plunged to the bottom.

My uncle, having been under the raft when he tipped it over, had no idea exactly where I had landed.

Panic began to settle in, no longer able to hold my breath, as I struggled to free myself from the slimy fingers of a large patch of seaweed in which I had become tangled.

In the midst of my struggle, a bright gold light shone down through the dark water and enveloped me. It was warm and safe, and the fear disappeared instantly.

I reached my arms up to the light and was lifted up into the very core of it. Being One with God was not a concept, but reality.

After going through this, one would assume a blessed life would follow. After all, I had been touched by God, and it wouldn't be the only time. He appeared to me again as a pillar of gold light in 2005. Within the light was swirling energy, and a voice emanated from it, imparting personal information before part of the light extended outward, entered my feet, and traveled upward throughout my entire body.

That night I believe I experienced what is termed *the Rapture.* Every cell was alive with God's energy. It was a heightened vibration that filled me, and was the most exquisite experience of my life.

I truly believe that had I not had these divine experiences, coupled with the visitations from Jesus that began at the age of five, and then my guiding angel, Grace, also having made her first appearance when I was five, I would not have been able to endure the dark path that my life would follow.

The first time Jesus came to me He filled me with an essence of enduring love that carried me through many challenges. But in spite of the ongoing visitations, my life, up until recently, seemed anything but blessed.

I had a very difficult childhood. Actually difficult is putting it mildly. Horrific is a more accurate description. I witnessed the total misuse of power, and was catapulted into an existence where evil reigned. Most of my past could be considered a horror story.

I created quite a bit of drama in my life, and it is truly a miracle that I am alive today. I narrowly escaped a third DE, having been attacked and nearly beaten to death in my thirties. I also manifested several forms of cancer, which was miraculously healed by the Philippine psychic surgeon, Alex Orbito, who I adore.

I can typically heal myself, but I was clearly guided to see Rev. Orbito, and I'm so glad I did. It was an amazing experience, and I have considered him a friend ever since.

He travels extensively with his work, usually in Europe. I visited him a few years ago in Vienna, and on the way home I had to change planes in New York. As I was headed for security I fell, hard, on both knees on the concrete floor. The pain was excruciating.

I laid there, literally writhing in pain as other travelers either stepped over or around me. It was a harsh realization of just how uncaring, or perhaps unconscious some people can be.

Finally a security guard came over as I tried to get up. Without an ounce of kindness he asked if I wanted to go to the hospital. I told him no, but I was going to need a wheelchair to get to the gate.

So, wheelchair bound, I was whisked off to go through security. The female TSA officer there demanded that I stand up so that she could pat me down.

The woman pushing the wheelchair was stunned, and explained my situation, telling the officer that I could not be expected to stand. But it was a useless effort.

So I pulled myself up and tolerated the abuse.

Due to the amount of extreme swelling and discoloration, I assumed I had broken both knee-caps. I sat on the plane for over five hours with nothing but ice packs for help. And I never once thought to lay hands on myself! I had become totally lost in the drama. I was in a bit of a state of shock, due to both the agony, and the lack of compassion. None of the flight attendants asked how I was, or if I needed anything during the duration of the flight.

I refused to do anything medically, and it wasn't until a day later, after pulling myself around on my rear-end because I couldn't walk, that a friend commented, "You have been doing healings on yourself, right?"

I felt absolutely dumbfounded. What had happened to my ability to think clearly? I had simply become so caught up in the drama that I lost all common sense.

I immediately did a healing on both knees, and within two days I was walking, and with only minimal discomfort.

At another time, after having taken a fall in my front yard and dislocating my elbow one evening, I was healed by an unseen force in the middle of the night.

Once again, I chose to forego medical attention. I could not fathom the idea of having it put back in place the way it is normally done, with force.

When I went to bed that night I was in a great deal of discomfort. I tried relieving the pain myself, but was not completely successful. But I had a peaceful feeling, as if there was nothing to worry about.

A couple of hours later I awoke, sensing someone was in my room, next to the bed. I looked around, but could see no one.

A euphoric feeling came over me as I lay there. This may sound odd, but I felt loved.

Then suddenly my arm began to move. It lifted slightly, and the bone was quickly repositioned. I felt nothing at all. The next morning it was as if I had never been injured.

I cannot say who it was that healed me that night, which is unusual after experiencing so many visitations where divine beings appear. I simply gave thanks for the love, and to whomever it was.

Besides experiencing ongoing visitations, I have heard the voices of the Creator, Jesus, and Grace for the majority of my life, since childhood. Voices of divine beings carry a particular vibration that is unique to each. In fact, so do their forms when they appear. Every divine being that has appeared to me emits such a high vibrational frequency that I become engulfed in it, totally caught up in a feeling of bliss.

The voices do not actually express in words. The message is being sent through vibrational streams of thought, and I am interpreting those thoughts and translating them into words. Often a message manifests as a vision.

I have had many visions in my lifetime. For me, it is often like watching a movie. It is through visions that I write my novels. I never plan to write. I just wait for the visions to begin.

Prior to writing my first novel, **Born of Betrayal**, I had a visitation from Archangel Michael. He projected a ray of light into my forehead, and the very next day I began having visions of people in another time and place. I went into seclusion and the book was completed in just 33 days.

Through the years I have received many messages. Some have been from God, guiding me in many ways, teaching me to overcome my past and create a decent life for myself. Jesus also has taught me many things, appearing in both physical form and in dreams. Grace would be the one to teach me a great deal about healing energy. Ultimately, I learned that no matter how many messages or visitations, it was up to me to cultivate my own inherent power in order to overcome the darkness.

And with every lesson I learned I always felt that a vital piece of information, *the key*, was yet to be given. I waited years for it.

It was first shown to me in a dream as a gold object. It was a very lengthy dream; one in which God spoke to me about my personal destiny. At the end of the dream I was standing in a grassy area next to a type of ashram. It was dark out; pitch black. I was looking down at something shiny, partially hidden in the blades of grass. I bent to pick it up and discovered a very large gold key. I knew it was sacred, and felt I had happened across something I shouldn't have touched.

I quickly put it back, and heard God say, "The key belongs to you."

From that time on I had yearned for its meaning, knowing that it would bring together all of the pieces of knowledge I had previously gained regarding energy.

Sometimes it's hard for me to believe how long it has taken me to reach the final phase, grasping the understanding necessary to become a true alchemist; not only utilizing the power in my work, but also my personal life. Only recently, at nearly 60 years of age, have I finally been given the meaning of *the key*, and I have used it extensively. I apply the principles every day, and I believe you will too. You will want to, because when you witness the positive changes that will begin to occur immediately, you won't have the desire to experience one day without utilizing them.

There was a period of time recently where my schedule became very hectic, and I missed three consecutive days of practicing the principles. I felt off. I did not feel as uplifted as I have come to enjoy regularly. Realizing the cause, the very next morning I got back on track, had a complete attitude adjustment, and felt thoroughly centered.

11

In this book I will share only the personal stories, messages, and teachings that are pertinent in helping you to understand *The Key* principles, allowing you to create a blessed life for yourself, if you apply them. And you are going to be amazed at how simple it is!

To utilize *The Key,* all that is required is a deep understanding in these four areas: The nature of Universal energy, the concept of time as it relates to energy, how your thoughts, emotions, and choices affect your energy, and therefore your reality, and finally, the true power that you hold. Then all you need to do is follow three simple steps, dedicating as little as a few minutes of your time every morning.

I would imagine that when you first laid eyes upon this book you may have wondered why it consists of so few pages, and only five short chapters. When I first began to write it I had intended to include my memoirs, sharing much of my life experiences, and more of the messages and teachings that I received throughout my life, which would have made it a much longer read; one that I thought would be meaningful. I wrote for two weeks, and though the book seemed to be turning out great, I physically felt drained. Something wasn't right. Then one night I had an epiphany: This book is not about me. It's about you. And my delving so deeply into my past was going against the principles of *The Key*. So I decided to forego the novel approach and simply give you what you need in a very simple, short package that would not require a huge investment of your time. And I am only sharing the parts of my life that I feel serve a purpose for you.

I believe that within these pages you will find many gifts. And when you are finished reading and understand *The Key,* and how to use it, I hope you will share it with others. I believe this information can unlock every door that has kept you from living the life you deserve.

1: Universal Energy

UNIVERSAL ENERGY

U niversal energy in our physical reality is everywhere. There is no place that it isn't. It is always moving, and is the force behind everything that is created. It moves in waves that vibrate at different rates of speed that are called frequencies.

Everything is made up of energy; even solid objects. All matter is made of molecules and space, and atoms that are vibrating at a certain frequency that make objects appear solid.

Universal energy does not think, it does not discern or judge. It only responds. And what it responds to is the energy being emitted from every living thing.

There is personal energy, and collective energy, both of which affect our lives. Right now, in my opinion, collective energy is a total mess, and that is why the world is in such a sad state of affairs. And we are all responsible, because our personal energy, as a whole, is a mess. This is due to being out of alignment with our non-physical reality: Source energy; Love, or that which we call God. And the mess is being projected into the Universe and creating our global reality.

However, when you live your life according to the guidelines in this book you are less affected by collective energy. You are able to remain stable no matter what is going on in the world around you. And as each of us raises the vibrational frequency of our own personal energy, we literally change the world.

The saying, "What goes around comes around," contains a tremendous amount of truth. All that you are experiencing is a result of an exchange of energy.

Vibrational frequencies are electromagnetic; an interrelation of electric currents and magnetic fields. We are all emitting currents and magnetizing like energy.

Every emotion and every thought carries a vibrational frequency, and when this frequency is emitted from within, into the Universal flow, the Universe delivers back to you more of the same.

How often have you heard someone say, or perhaps even said yourself, "I have the worst luck?" Many times I've heard people complain about how *unlucky* they are in love. Sometimes out of frustration at something not going right, the phrase is, "Just my luck." And at times when things do go right, the perception may be that luck is behind it. There is a difference between the illusion of being lucky, and the reality of being blessed. The outcome of your choices has absolutely nothing to do with luck, and nothing happens by chance. The outcome has everything to do with your energy, and the exchange you are having with Universal energy.

Low frequencies have a negative charge. High frequencies have a positive charge. If your thoughts and emotions are centered around your troubles, you are emitting a very negative charge because the frequency is very low. In turn, the Universe flows back to you more negative energy, a low frequency with which to create from. And so you will feel stuck in your current situation, unable to break free of the negative cycle, wondering what you are doing wrong.

Throughout my life I could not understand why I wasn't further along. No matter how hard I tried I just could not seem to move forward in a way that I desired, and felt I should. In dedicating my life to doing God's work and helping so many people, I felt my rewards would be great. This is not to say that there were no rewards, just that I wasn't recognizing them. And I could only go so far because I was dwelling heavily on my past, concentrating on the negative events, feeling hurt, disappointed, and angry; a prisoner of circumstance.

Carrying around that negative vibration was not allowing me to fully embrace and manifest my true worth.

When working with clients I have seen amazing results over and over. When performing a healing I impart a very high vibrational frequency through my hands. My mind is centered in positive thoughts, and I see the energy that is within the body of the client, which is revealed in waves, patterns, and colors. Disease carries a very low vibrational frequency, so as the higher frequency enters, it dispels the lower. You can actually hear sounds of static electricity as I manipulate the energy.

Besides healing the sick, I also perform energy clearings, where I am able to remove or dispel negative energy and blockages that have resulted from the drama and trauma of one's life. Negative energy accumulates through life, and unless it is released, it can wreak havoc.

Many believe, that because there is negative energy stored somewhere in your energetic field that this means you are a bad person. Not necessarily so. Some of the very best people are carrying the weight of negative energy.

It also does not mean that you are weak. You simply cannot operate in your full power when negative energy is present within you.

I have witnessed people's lives change for the better overnight once their energy is balanced. But I have learned that in order to keep one's energy clear it is important to allow emotions to flow unhindered. All emotions help us to maintain balance. But from an early age we are typically conditioned not to feel. We are told, "Don't cry, don't be angry." So we begin to suppress our feelings. And then we go through life wondering why we have difficulties in relationships, communication, challenges with work, health, self esteem, and the ability to truly love ourselves.

Emotions are *energy in motion*. So it is important for emotions to flow. Otherwise emotional health is challenged, mental processes are affected, and ultimately the physical body will suffer the consequences. All suppressed emotions can become destructive.

Even anger must be expressed. If it isn't, it turns to rage. Expressing anger does not have to be a bad thing. There are healthy ways to express anger, and all other emotions through conscious communication.

Think before you speak, and consider the possible outcome of your words before you speak them. Most people have no idea how to communicate in a healthy way. Expression becomes distorted, and words tend to inflict pain.

Working with *The Key* principles helps to dispel the negativity that has accumulated over the years, and health is easier to maintain. Those principles revolve around re-programming your thinking. Understanding how energy is at work in your life will help you to re-pattern your thought processes, enabling you to create the perfect life for you.

2: TODAY

TODAY

The possibilities that lay before you are limitless. Besides manifesting a wonderful life, you will eventually be able to heal your own body because a sick body manifests from toxic thoughts. Again, in re-programming your thinking, which is what *The Key* entails, you should only manifest health in all areas of your life – mental, emotional, physical, and spiritual. Your life can be enriched in every way, and you can experience peace.

The mind can heal when you learn to center your thoughts in the present, and in one particular area, which will be introduced in chapter five. (Don't peek!)

In creating a blessed life you must choose to relinquish your attachment to all aspects of your past, and all perceptions of your future. And you must choose change. The kind of positive change that you desire can only be accomplished by focusing your attention on only today. Otherwise you are living in limitation.

Jesus once gave me a very powerful message regarding living only for today. It happened in 1996, the year after I had written ***Born of Betrayal***. The experience of writing the book was life-changing in many ways. My senses had become heightened, and I found it hard to be in public. I was much more comfortable then, and in several years to come, living a very reclusive life.

I was renting a very small apartment in Del Mar, California. I supported my meager existence performing healings once in a while, but I was living month-to-month financially.

I woke up one morning hearing a song from the Broadway play *Annie*. I had always had an aversion to the song *Tomorrow* without any particular reason. I just couldn't tolerate it.

So I was a bit confused as the words, "Tomorrow, tomorrow, I love ya tomorrow. You're only a day away," resounded in my head.

I sat up, hands cupped over my ears, as I said aloud, "I can't stand that song!"

I immediately heard the voice of Jesus. He said, "Isn't it interesting? Tomorrow never comes. It's always today."

It truly is always today, and today is the only space of time in which you can create. Nothing exists outside of today; only memories of the past and thoughts of an illusionary future.

The past is nowhere. The future is nowhere. Neither possesses an energy frequency from which to create because it doesn't exist. Universal energy does not recognize it, so it cannot respond to it.

Life is only happening now. Where there is no life-force, there is no energy. Only in the present is there life-force energy, so only in the present is there creative power.

No matter how good or bad your memories make you feel, you will have no power with which to create if your thoughts are centered anywhere but the here and now. So you feel stuck, like glue, in Nowhere Land.

With positive creation, there is a particular feeling that must be generated, which will also be revealed in chapter five, that can only truly be experienced through thoughts that are based in reality; what actually exists today.

This does not mean that you should never talk about, or think about your past or your aspirations for the future. It's really impossible not to unless you are suffering from amnesia! Just realize that you are not in a creative mode when you do.

Also, when you have a negative emotional attachment to any memories, or thoughts regarding your future, you are holding on *today* to a low vibrational frequency that will result in fatigue. What you focus on will either enrich or deplete you physically.

The results of the past should only ever be the lessons learned, and it is important to be grateful for the lessons as they come, no matter how they manifest. In every experience there is a lesson in empowerment to be obtained.

I have personally chosen to allow my past to serve a greater purpose. The experiences have taught me so much, and they have molded and shaped me into the person that I am today, and I like who I am. So I am able to carry the lessons with me while leaving everything else behind.

Unfortunately, some people are so lost in victimization that they cannot even admit there might actually be a lesson, or even a gift. Often the lesson or gift may need to be discovered in order to let go and move on, and by embracing it, healing can occur.

For most people, even if their thoughts are focused on what is happening in the present, those thoughts are usually not being fueled properly. And typically they are thinking about today's problems, thus creating more negativity.

When practicing *The Key* principles, your attention must be centered on today. The more you exercise the principles the less you will want to ponder on the past, or the future. You will find more comfort staying present.

Letting go of the past is easier if you simply direct your thoughts away from it and focus on today. If you can focus on only today, worries are less likely to invade your mind. And when it comes right down to it, isn't today enough? Sometimes it's more than enough.

3: THE CHOICE TO CHANGE

THE CHOICE TO CHANGE

T aking responsibility for your life is a vital step. You cannot experience change until you choose to accept responsibility for being the sole architect of your current reality.

Change can only come when you realize that you are not a victim. Now this may be hard for some to perceive because there is a part of you that cannot comprehend that you are not a victim of the circumstances of your life. But you are, in fact, totally responsible for the circumstances of your life. You have drawn to you every experience from within, which is the energy being emitted into the Universe. You have attracted it all.

Each soul comes in to this incarnation with an agenda. I call this *destiny*. Optimally, we will attract the types of experiences that allow us to fulfill our intention. Unfortunately, our choices often leave us unfulfilled.

When you realize that you have powerfully shaped your reality, no matter what that consists of, and are continuing to do so, and you can release your attachment to victimization, you open up to change.

If your current reality is not all that you desire, which it must not be or you would not be reading this book, it is because you are tapped in to a fear-based negative vibrational frequency, and are projecting from that place. This does not necessarily mean that you are a negative person. You may be the most joyful, fun, loving person in the world. It does not mean that you aren't a negative person either. Either way, there is a negative stream of energy that you are manifesting from.

Negative energy is the effect of negative thinking and/or holding on to negative emotions. Projecting negative thoughts toward others, suppressing emotions resulting from trauma, or harboring feelings such as jealousy, regret, or guilt, can be self-destructive. These types of thoughts and feelings create a chain of negative experiences. And when you want someone else to experience negative emotions such as guilt, you are actually causing yourself harm.

There is a tendency for most people to become lost in negativity when their life is miserable. It is a vicious cycle that is difficult to overcome, and understandably so. I was one of those people.

Some people say they want change, but they are actually quite attached to suffering. It is very easy to become attached to the drama and trauma of one's life, and to the drama of other people's lives. And it is often more comfortable to stay rooted in old patterns than it is to welcome change.

Many people find excuses not to change. Those excuses are most often based on past events and experiences. Perhaps you were abused as a child, or come from a broken home, or had alcoholic parents. You may have erected a wall of protection in order to shield yourself from ever being hurt again. In truth, you are living in a prison cell. Whatever the case may be, there is absolutely no excuse that is good enough to keep change from happening in your life. You can free yourself by choosing forgiveness.

Forgiveness has been a misperceived subject. True forgiveness does not mean condoning inappropriate behavior. Forgiveness is the act of letting go of the experiences of the past, acknowledging the lessons, and giving thanks for those lessons. I believe that *The Key* can help you to do that, and it will, in time, become natural.

One common statement that has always disturbed me, and to me is really a cop-out, is, "I have no choice." There is *always* choice. But what you may be lacking is either the belief that you can change, or the willpower to change. If either is the case, you must ask yourself why belief and willpower are lacking. The answer will usually be connected to the past.

I am not making light of anyone's situation, and quite honestly *The Key* may be easier for some than others to benefit from, and some may not be ready to surrender and do the work. It requires commitment, though minimal. Regardless, it can be difficult to release blame, assume responsibility, and take charge of one's life.

Over the years I have witnessed so many miracles with my healing work. But I have also seen some reject the blessing for one reason or another.

One man was not willing to give up his disability check in exchange for being healed. Another found comfort in the attention he was getting. One young man who was paralyzed from the waist down had built his home with wheelchair accessibility in most rooms, and could not reconcile himself with letting go of the expense he had invested, only to have it become unnecessary if he were healed. A young lady came once with a back injury due to a car accident, and she was hoping for a financial settlement. She realized, that until she received it, she could not let go of the pain.

I'm sure your reaction to these scenarios is one of disbelief. Personally I can't imagine turning away from wellness. But many do.

Often sickness is manifested as a way out; a way out of doing something undesired, or even a way out of this incarnation. Can you recall a time when you've gotten ill when you had something to do that you really didn't want to do at all? Then you say, with disappointment, "Just my luck!"

Often through suffering there are lessons and gifts to be discovered if we just search for them. And we can utilize those lessons to avoid future suffering.

Years ago there was a woman who had been suffering with widespread pain and an autoimmune disorder due to toxicity after her breast implants had ruptured.

She was able to drag herself out of bed one afternoon and come for a healing. But before I began I told her we needed to have a chat. She had become involved in a civil lawsuit and was one of the people heading up the campaign for other women who were suffering the same fate.

I told her that I was aware of her position, and asked how she would feel, if in forty-five minutes, she was well. She needed to question how being healed would affect her crusade.

She immediately began to cry. She actually hadn't thought how being healed would change the path she was on.

I felt so much compassion for her, and told her that no matter what her choice was, I would not judge it. I then left her alone to contemplate her situation and make her choice.

When I returned twenty minutes later there were no tears, only firm resolve. She stated that she wanted to be healed. And she was.

I saw her a few weeks later at a social gathering and she was the picture of perfect health. She told me that she had dropped out of the lawsuit, given up her position in the campaign, and wished all the other women well, but she was moving on with her life. She had powerfully chosen change, and the results were amazing.

It is so important to never lose a sense of compassion for what others are going through, to be supportive, and offer help when it's appropriate. But never lose yourself in the drama of another person's experiences, binding yourself to it energetically, or to traumatic global events. It is not beneficial.

How often have you become lost in another person's problems, or found yourself glued to the television when a negative event has occurred, watching the shocking details over and over?

Ask yourself if you truly want change. Envision your life without all the negativity and drama. How does it make you feel? Are you comfortable not engaging with other people's dramatic events? Some people enjoy it. Some people like drama. Do you?

This is the place where we begin. Only move on to chapter four if you are willing to accept responsibility for your own energy, and are willing to learn how to dissolve the negative, and begin to operate from a healthy vibration.

4: YOUR INHERENT POWER

YOUR INHERENT POWER

T he first step to creating the life you desire is to realize the power that lies within. You have tremendous power. All that you require are the tools with which to channel that power; tools that I will provide.

Before we go any further it is important to understand the inherent power that you hold. In order to comprehend it, you need to understand your connection to divine power.

When I say *divine power*, I am referring to the Creator, Who I am most comfortable calling God, or Source energy.

You are One with the Creator energetically. There is no separation. There is a direct connection. You are actually an extension of the energy that is the Source of all creation. In essence, you are an aspect of Love, and with that comes the ability to create, which is why you are here.

I imagine that this statement may make a lot of people uncomfortable. If so, it is because you are not used to claiming and owning who you are spiritually.

I once asked God to give me a vision of the oneness that exists, and the vision that I received was of a giant ball of gold light similar to the sun. There were billions of rays of light emanating from the core. Each of those rays, our souls, are interconnected through that central Source that is the pure vibration of Love. In understanding this you can see how we are all One.

Within our energetic field there are emotional centers we term *chakras*, the solar plexus being what I call the *power center*, referring to self-empowerment. The solar plexus is located in the back of the stomach, in front of the aorta, just below the diaphragm. It is the largest autonomic nerve center in the abdominal cavity.

Some refer to this area as the pit of the stomach. When referring to intuition, some say they feel it in their gut. When performing energy clearings, I find this area to be most affected negatively. This is because humans do not recognize that they are not purely physical. The non-physical aspect is overlooked. And it is from the non-physical connection to Source that our power stems.

Jesus taught that the Kingdom is inside you. You are centered in God. God is centered in you. This connection to the divine is what allows you to create at all. Your life-force energy flows from Source, and radiates throughout your entire being; energy that most, throughout the course of their lives have tainted with chaotic thinking.

You are the Creator of your reality. You are creating everything that is happening now, everything that has ever happened, and everything that will happen, right now! When you recognize this to be true you can no longer remain a victim. Your thoughts in relation to the past, present, and future are generating emotions that are generating energy. Where those thoughts are focused determines what you will create. The choice is yours to dwell in misery, or powerfully create bliss. Only you can shape your NOW.

5: THE KEY

THE KEY

Y ou can now free yourself. The *key* is *gratitude*. Gratitude possesses the power to fulfill every want and need. But wants and needs will not be your focus when exercising *The Key* principles.

Wanting and needing suggests lack, so when you say, "I want," or "I need," you are emitting a frequency of lack, and the Universe sends you what? Nothing. It cannot project any energy your way from which to manifest.

Many of you most likely have delved into the realm of gratitude already. Many work with principles of positive thinking. Both have been subjects of great attention for years. You may even have a gratitude journal. You might give thanks every day for one thing or another. But creating goes beyond positive thinking, and there are guidelines involved that one must follow in order to see the most positive results of gratefulness.

The greatest benefits cannot be realized through an exercise in simply reciting or writing a list of the things you appreciate. It goes much deeper than that.

Your gratitude must generate a feeling within. That particular feeling is contentment. When you are content you are *not* emitting a vibration of lack. Contentment carries an extremely high vibration, and is a powerful ally when working in partnership with gratitude.

Love is the highest vibration that exists. It is the essence of who you are. It is your inherent power. When you give thanks, you are acknowledging that you are blessed. You are acknowledging that Love is at work in your life. When you acknowledge your blessings, and *feel* the depth of your gratitude, the Universe reciprocates, sending you the most powerful vibrational frequencies of gratitude, contentment, and Love, from which to create a life of positive abundance effortlessly. Focusing on blessings helps you disengage from the negative stream of fear-based energy and helps you tune in to the positive frequency of Source energy.

As you participate, you may find yourself giving thanks for some of the same things every day, and it may feel repetitive. It doesn't matter. As you do this there will be additional blessings you will become conscious of. It isn't *what* you are giving thanks for that matters, or how many things you are grateful for, only that you are grateful for something, and generating a feeling of contentment.

Everyone has *something* to be grateful for, no matter how bad their current situation may be. Be grateful that the sun is shining, that you have a roof over your head, or that you have eyes to see. There simply is no excuse not to participate.

It may be harder for some to generate a feeling of contentment because their lives are severely challenged, but it can be accomplished if one understands the information that has been given.

It is important to understand that, if for instance, you are giving thanks that you have enough money in the bank today to pay your bills, it doesn't mean that when Universal energy responds that you will manifest more monetary blessings. It doesn't mean that you won't either. You cannot control how your blessings will present themselves. Just know that they will. And without concentrating on your wants and needs, they will naturally be met. Enjoy the surprises as they show up at the perfect moment, and give thanks when they do.

Not all of the blessings you generate will be life-changing. Some may be seen in the little things such as a stranger being exceptionally kind, or a visit from a friend that brought enjoyment. Perhaps a co-worker that you had previously had issues with suddenly directs a smile your way, or a business meeting turns out far better than anticipated. A blessing may reveal itself as an auto shop, visible right across the street just as the *low oil* light illuminates and you're forty miles away from home, which happened to me recently. The mechanic didn't even charge me for the two quarts of oil needed.

There are so many blessings that get overlooked in the course of one day. But you will begin to be more aware of them, and when you give thanks in the moment when they occur, you will generate even more positive Universal energy flowing your way.

When I was first guided to begin, God said to just allow myself thirty seconds to contemplate on what I am grateful for. Easier said than done!

Upon waking, I closed my eyes again, took a deep breath, and the first thing that popped into my mind was how grateful I was to be lying in such a comfortable bed. And it dawned on me how I had taken that for granted, as well as a host of other comforts that exist in my life. I began to recognize, in that short span of time, how truly blessed I am.

Thirty seconds extended to thirty minutes as I continued to give thanks for so many things I had previously taken for granted. And I could have gone on for a much longer period of time.

Soon, a feeling welled up inside of me. I felt it deep down in my core, right in my solar plexus. It felt so good. It was a feeling of being content.

That day turned out to be the best day I had had in a long time. And since that day I have been blessed in so many ways that I have come to expect daily blessings. Living in gratitude and reaping the benefits has become a natural way to live. I'm personally finding that since being given *the key* I am drawing to me what is essential and supportive in creating the life I deserve.

Will there still be bumps in the road? Perhaps. That is because you can't change the way other people behave and react, but you can change the way in which you respond. You should find you are dealing with matters in a healthier way because you are unaffected by what is going on outside of you. You will not find the pull to engage in drama because you are content. Also, as you begin to emit a frequency of contentment, people will feel that, and not be so inclined to stir up altercations.

You are now ready to begin to create consciously. The following guidelines consist of three steps. Practice these steps every day in order to experience maximum benefits.

THE KEY GUIDELINES

ONE

The way to begin is to start your day focusing on something you're grateful for. This can take as little as a few minutes, or as long as you like. I know that most everyone has time constraints, especially in the morning. But I truly believe you can set that alarm five minutes earlier in order to participate in changing your life.

It is vital that you do this upon waking because when you sleep you are not generating a momentum of energy that Universal energy will respond to. You are basically in a null-zone. Your thought processes are not active in the same way as when you are awake. A null-zone is without value, effect, consequence, or significance vibrationally. The moment you wake your conscious thought processes begin, and it is from your thinking, and the feelings your thinking generates, that creation manifests.

Typically as soon as you awaken, your thoughts are in multiple places at once, which is chaotic. And typically those thoughts are immediately focused on any challenges that may exist.

We don't want thoughts straying to any area other than gratitude. It is important to generate a positive creative vibrational frequency that sets the course for the day ahead. When you begin your day in gratitude, you do just that.

Remember, when you feel content you attract more positive energy from which to manifest, and your contentment grows. When you acknowledge your blessings in this way you will realize more and more blessings are showing up in your life. And it is important, that in the moment those blessings are revealed, that you give thanks as soon as they are realized, generating more positive creative energy.

You can focus on one thing you're grateful for, or a hundred things. It really doesn't matter, as long as you're generating a feeling of contentment.

The more you participate, the more natural it will become, and you will find yourself giving thanks throughout the day, not just in the morning. This is a form of conscious living.

You must do this every morning to obtain optimum results. And always finish by saying, "I am *so* blessed. I am *truly, truly* blessed!"

Defined, the word *so* means *"to a great extent"*, and *truly* means *"to the fullest degree"*. These two words will carry a high vibration and have a positive emotional charge when focusing on blessings and said with feeling.

TWO

Only be grateful for what you *have* now, whether it be material things, relationships, your health, this book! Seriously, you will find an endless list of blessings to give thanks for.

Only give thanks for what is *happening* now. To create, you cannot give thanks for something that occurred yesterday, or what might happen tomorrow. Remember, the Universe cannot respond.

If your thoughts wander outside of today just re-center them and continue.

THREE

If at some point a challenge arises during the course of the day, pause, take a breath, and focus your thoughts on one thing that you're grateful for. As you center yourself in contentment, it will shift the current dynamic.

CONCLUSION

That's it! Three easy steps. Pretty simple. So there is no reason not to begin to utilize *The Key.*

Do not expect your whole life to change in one day. Give it time. Put forth your daily efforts, and you should begin to notice positive changes right away. I certainly did.

When I say *efforts,* I mean that you still have to live life. Move forward with ideas and endeavors, and pay attention to opportunities.

There should be immediate shifts in your overall sense of well-being, and the blessings being created will be realized. Each and every day that you participate should only get better and better. You have tapped in to an endless stream of power in which to create your perfect existence.

You should also begin to feel more energized. I have noticed that if I don't get ample sleep due to long hours of work, I still feel energized the following day because I'm content.

I believe that eventually, as the mind becomes more and more aligned with Source, with thoughts focused in gratitude, and contentment grows, physical ailments become less and less a part of your reality. You are learning to relax, realizing that everything is in divine order. *Divine order* means that all is being perfectly arranged by the inherent power within you. With this comes a reduction in stress, which will certainly benefit the body.

Your cells are responding to your thoughts and emotions, thus changing every moment as a result. When you realize you have powerfully manifested sickness out of negative thoughts and emotions, you also realize that you can just a powerfully create wellness out of positive thoughts and emotions.

I suppose it is safe to say that in following the guidelines in this book you are learning a new way to pray. Typically prayer includes asking a higher power for what you want and need. Some people only pray in times of great need, and will even barter with God. Many times those prayers are answered. But how many of you have felt frustrated because you have asked and asked, and have not received? And then you are left wondering why.

I am suggesting that you *never* ask for a blessing. Just as wants and needs, asking projects an energy of lack. Instead, give thanks that you and your loved ones are truly, truly blessed.

Most of us have been in situations where it is not easy to remain calm, especially when the well-being of loved ones are concerned. We will literally beg God to intervene on their behalf.

I have always said that God knows what is in my heart. Our connection goes beyond words. God knows exactly what you feel, what you want, and what you need. It is not necessary to beg.

The words I say every time I perform a healing are: "I give thanks to you, beloved Creator, for shining your light upon this person, and blessing them with your love."

These words of prayer come from a place of faith rather than desperation, which is fear-based. I am acknowledging the power that is already at work.

True gratitude, in general, is lacking in the world. Greed, unfortunately, is a driving force that is adding to the collective fear-based energy field. Greed carries a very low vibrational frequency, almost as low as fear, which is the lowest, so only negativity can manifest globally.

I endeavor every day to grow, and to become a better version of myself. *The Key* has changed my life, and I believe that it will continue to. Because of it, my life can only improve, and I believe the same will be true for you.

Remember, what you think about and how you feel will always line up vibrationally with what you create.

So please do your part, and perhaps, individually, as we utilize our inherent power and direct out thoughts constructively, we can make a difference; not only personally, but globally. No matter what, you now have the power to create your own piece of Heaven right here on Earth.

ABOUT LACEY

LACEY HAWK is a faith healer and author. She has written two novels, *Born of Betrayal,* which has been adapted for the screen, and the sequel, *Beyond Forgiveness*.

Her children's book, *Maximilian, the Most Handsome Kitten in the World* is in the process of being published, and is scheduled to be available in bookstores by Christmas 2015.

She continues to see clients, performing healings and energy clearings world-wide, in person and remotely. She is available for spiritual counseling, both in person and on the phone.

Lacey currently resides in Las Vegas, Nevada.

More information is available on Lacey's website:
www.laceyhawk.com

Please feel free to email her at: ofinnerpeace@aol.com

NOTES

NOTES